T0246529

AWAKE and ALIVE

AWAKE
and ALIVE

Thomas Merton
According to His
Novices

Edited by Jon M. Sweeney
With photographs by Paul Quenon, OCSO

ORBIS BOOKS
Maryknoll, New York 10545

Founded in 1970, Orbis Books endeavors to publish works that enlighten the mind, nourish the spirit, and challenge the conscience. The publishing arm of the Maryknoll Fathers and Brothers, Orbis seeks to explore the global dimensions of the Christian faith and mission, to invite dialogue with diverse cultures and religious traditions, and to serve the cause of reconciliation and peace. The books published reflect the views of their authors and do not represent the official position of the Maryknoll Society. To learn more about Maryknoll and Orbis Books, please visit our website at www.orbisbooks.com

Library of Congress Cataloging-in-Publication Data

Names: Sweeney, Jon M., 1967- editor.
Title: Awake and Alive : Thomas Merton according to his novices /
    edited by Jon M. Sweeney ; with photographs by Paul Queron, OCSO.
Description: Maryknoll, New York : Orbis Books, [2022] | Includes
    bibliographical references. | Summary: "The personality and spiritual
    practices of Thomas Merton, revealed by fellow monks who knew him
    best"—Provided by publisher.
Identifiers: LCCN 2022003273 (print) | LCCN 2022003274 (ebook) |
    ISBN 9781626984912 (hardcover) | ISBN 9781608339532 (epub)
Subjects: LCSH: Merton, Thomas, 1915-1968—Anecdotes. | Trappists. |
    Monks—United States—Anecdotes. | Spiritual life—Catholic Church.
Classification: LCC BX4705.M542 W39 2022 (print) |
LCC BX4705.M542 (ebook) | DDC 206/.57—dc23/eng/20220511
LC record available at https://lccn.loc.gov/2022003273
LC ebook record available at https://lccn.loc.gov/2022003274

For every monk,
and every monk in the world

Contents

Introduction

Thomas Merton wore many hats. As a writer, he was a poet, an autobiographer and memoirist, hagiographer, essayist, diarist, and author of one of the richest bodies of correspondence of any twentieth-century literary figure. Most importantly, he wrote several of the classic works of Christian spirituality of his era—the latter twentieth century—including *The Seven Storey Mountain, New Seeds of Contemplation, Zen and the Birds of Appetite, The Way of Chuang Tzu,* and *Conjectures of a Guilty Bystander.*

As a human being, Merton was an artist and prophetic voice on war, race, and the issues of the day, and an encourager of like-minded artists and activists throughout the world. His friends and correspondents included the cofounder of the Catholic Worker Movement, Dorothy Day; the Lithuanian-born Polish poet living in California who eventually won the Nobel Prize in Literature, Czeslaw Milosz; an earlier Nobel winner, the Russian poet, novelist, and translator, Boris Pasternak; Nicaraguan poet and politician, Ernesto Cardenal, who in fact spent two years at the Abbey of Gethsemani with Merton as his Novice Master; and Fr. Daniel Berrigan SJ, who was often getting arrested in protests of the atrocities of the Vietnam War, with Merton's encouragement. There was also a long letter from Merton to the great novelist and civil rights champion, James Baldwin, which as far as we know went unanswered, and an intended gathering in April 1968 of Martin Luther King Jr. and Merton at the Abbey of Gethsemani, which never happened due to the assassination of Dr. King only a few days beforehand.

As a friend and mentor to others, he was also a student and teacher of Christian spirituality, Catholic mystics, and his own Cistercian religious tradition. And he was a mystic himself, actively discovering the spiritualities of Eastern religions, Indigenous traditions, Judaism, Sufism, pushing people in his own church to explore the truth of others, years before documents written at the Second Vatican Council made it "permissible" for Catholics to do so. He also had a gift for friendship, and was able to truly meet and know people of faith and wisdom around the world who sought him out.

But Merton was first and foremost a monk. And beside H. H. the Dalai Lama and Thich Nhat Hanh, both of whom Merton met in person, he is probably one of only three famous monks in modern history. As a monk, he served for a decade in his monastery in Kentucky, the Abbey of Gethsemani, as Novice Master, from 1955 to 1965, teaching young men studying to become Trappist monks. He was beloved in this role, and most of the stories and anecdotes that follow have been told by his former novices.

Four of the authors of these anecdotes were Merton's novices; two of them—Fr. Chrysogonus Waddell and Fr. John Eudes Bamberger—

were Scholastics when Merton was Novice Master.

In this book, you meet Thomas Merton as Novice Master and as monastic brother, confessor, spiritual director, and friend. Our title, *Awake and Alive*, is designed to reflect a way of being in the world, which is known to millions of readers of Merton's books. This way of being is distinguished by insight, awareness, and imagination. One of the reflections to come is from Brother Paul Quenon, who, speaking of Merton, reflects, "He was aware and awake and alive in his imagination and considered that to be an important part of his spiritual life. So, I've emulated that example." Abbot Timothy Kelly, OCSO later echoes Quenon (they were interviewed separately) when he remarks, "[He was] always really alive!"

It was Merton who first made the treasures of monastic life and monastic spirituality accessible to people outside the cloister. In many respects, what he did for his students at the Abbey of Gethsemani he did for those who read his books, heard his recorded lectures, and who continue today to follow his path. In this respect, becoming *Awake and Alive* is a path for all of us.

It is useful to remember the themes of Thomas Merton's life during the time period covered by these personal stories: the 1950s and 1960s.

Although he was always an enthusiastic teacher, and his students almost universally appreciated him, we also know that he was experiencing some inner conflict during his years as Novice Master, often wondering if he was guiding young men to become something that he wasn't himself fully sure that he wanted to be. For instance, Merton at times seriously considered leaving Gethsemani to become a Carthusian hermit. He would have more solitude and time for contemplative practice as a Carthusian. But "Reverend Father [his Abbot, Dom James] threw buckets of cold water on the mere suggestion," he wrote in his journal on October 10, 1952.

A few months later, that same abbot gave Merton permission to begin spending periods of time in solitude and seclusion from the community of monks, and an old toolshed in the woods was identified as the place where he might first do this. Merton fixed it up a bit and named it St. Anne's. It was there that he wrote the book *Thoughts in Solitude*. In his journal on February 24, 1953, he writes, "[H]ere at St. Anne's I am always happy and at peace no matter what happens. For there is no need for anyone but God." But the desire to leave Gethsemani for a different kind of monastic life kept coming back to him. In the summer of 1957 he confided, "The hope of a monastery in Ecuador. . . . Is it a hope or a temptation? . . . (All the time my stomach is sick with the feeling that with Dom James nothing of the sort is possible.)"[1]

It has been reasonably suggested that the Abbot then gave his restless, brilliant monk, Father Louis (Merton's monastic name), the job of Master of Novices to slow him down and to center him in a monk's work. It was also a job that Merton was very qualified to do. He was responsible for training the young men, teaching them the classics of Christian theology, and of Cistercian history and spirituality. He seems to have relished this responsibility. He was also to see that the men followed a healthy pattern of personal prayer and meditation as well as development of character. This is a job for an experienced monk, who is also a priest, and who can work well with his Abbot.

Merton's lectures to the monks were a bit unorthodox in the range of material he presented. Through Merton, novices were exposed to more than theological and spiritual classics, but also to modern writers of fiction, such as William Faulkner, and contemporary poets, such as Boris Pasternak. This is notable because, in those days, a monk's reading material was only supposed to be of a "spiritual" kind. Novels were usually forbidden. Similarly, Merton the Novice Master's occasional comments on political issues of the day were offered fleetingly, but were nonetheless significant, since news of the outside world, for Trappists in the 1950s and 60s, was only to be shared with the monks by their Abbot. Abbots also usually instructed their monks how they were to vote when national elections came around.

Merton even talked with his novices about yoga, Native American spirituality, Buddhism, and the dramas of the unfolding Cold War. And he didn't restrict himself, or them, to only intellectual work; sometimes he led them in walks in the woods, or manual work with purpose, such as clearing tomato plants killed by a recent frost. He mostly reveled in the work, whatever its form, but over time, when the responsibility was taken from him, he was grateful to be done and to have more time to himself and his evolving vocation.

In *The Life You Save May Be Your Own*, an intertwining story of four great Catholic figures and writers of that time—Flannery O'Connor, Walker Percy, Dorothy Day, and Thomas Merton—Paul Elie expresses some of the paradoxes that Merton embodied just before 1960:

> [H]e had been a Catholic for twenty years and a Trappist monk for seventeen. He no longer saw the Abbey of Gethsemani as the center of his or anybody's existence. Set apart from the other monks by his background, his fame, his literary calling, and his yearning for solitude, he had come to see himself as an independent, a Trappist of Gethsemani whose real life was elsewhere. He no longer saw the outside world as a nest of vipers, but he didn't yearn to be out in the world making his way as a poet or a college professor, either. He had no desire to be anything but a monk. Rather, he felt called to be a monk on different terms—to be more intensely a monk than he was.[2]

This "sets the stage" for the stories, sayings, and anecdotes to come.

❧

Most of the content of these pages began as interviews conducted with six of Merton's former brother monks. All of them were novices under his direction. One was his secretary. One was his final Abbot, after Dom James retired. All six remained in the monastery—not always the Abbey of Gethsemani—for many decades, until the end of their lives, and each went on to become a notable monastic in his own right.

In pages 15–48, we have the voice of Brother Paul Quenon, OCSO.

In pages 49–64, we have the voice of Abbot Timothy Kelly, OCSO.

In pages 65–82, we have the voice of Father Chrysogonus Waddell, OCSO.

In pages 83–90, we have the voice of Father John Eudes Bamberger, OCSO.

In pages 91–116, we have the voice of Father Matthew Kelty, OCSO.

In pages 117–128, we have the voice of Father Flavian Burns, OCSO.

As one Trappist friend said to me recently, this collection might as well be called "Merton Apophthegmata," and that is true. The word *apophthegmata* is often used in connection with the Desert Fathers and Mothers of Christian antiquity, whom Merton adored, studied, and taught—the word meaning a collection of pithy maxims, stories, and sayings. Other significant figures in history, such as Plutarch and Erasmus, have also had their *apophthegmata* published.

For those readers who know Merton's life and his close monastic friends, the question may arise, why do we not have reflections from Brother Patrick Hart, OCSO, who was Merton's last personal secretary, here? The answer was offered to me by the director of the Thomas Merton Studies Center in Louisville: "Patrick always refused to do one [an interview about his time spent with Fr. Louis]. He always got very emotional when his relationship with Merton came up; I guess it dominated his life's work. I was working on him, and he seemed to be getting more amenable, but then his health began to decline" (Dr. Paul M. Pearson).[3]

May you find something to inspire you in what follows.

Jon M. Sweeney

Thomas Merton as Known by His Fellow Monks

Brother Paul Quenon, OCSO

My first meeting was in the retreat house. I was told that the Novice Master would come to meet me, and this rather heavy-set man, who seemed pretty old to me, came in. I figured he must be sixty-five, although actually he was only about forty-three at the time. He didn't ask too many questions. He didn't seem to be probing much. He seemed to be more interested in getting me into the flow of things. And he said, "Tomorrow we'll be going out in the woods and cutting down some trees." That visual way of talking was characteristic of him, and it should have been a clue right away that he was Thomas Merton, but I didn't recognize him. He was just the Novice Master to me.

Things went on for about a month, and I had no idea that the Novice Master was Thomas Merton until somebody told me. I was very happy it happened that way because by then I had established a relationship based on the fact that he was my Novice Master and not a famous writer, whom I had read already. That continued to be the nature of the relationship, and it was always in the forefront. Occasionally we might talk about something he'd written and maybe sometimes he would share something he had written. But it was very much a secondary thing.

It was more a disciple relationship—as a disciple rather than a relationship as a student—and there was a certain level of trust that you had to have and a kind of intimacy. You disclosed something of your own spiritual struggles, an opening of the heart, where you talked about how you think God is working in your life. Or what God wants for you, what is my vocation, do I really belong here? What has been my experience in growing up? These are all things that you have to discuss.

His manner was casual and practical. He would ask you how you were doing at work, what's it like in choir, how do you like choir, what'd you think of that talk in Chapter the other day. Just incidental things, what's going on in the monastery and what's going on in your life. You would go from there into deeper things.

The superficial conversation could go on for quite a while sometimes, and often it wasn't until near the end, when the bell was going to ring for Compline, that I would bring up something important. Then we would have to stay and miss Compline. I don't think he minded that too much. He said I would "bring the rabbit out of the hat at the very end," so that became a habit.

I found a lot of times that he could read my heart, and this is "discernment of spirit," which the Desert Fathers talk about.

He could read me in a way I couldn't read myself. He understood me better than I understood myself sometimes, and that was a bit unsettling. I certainly couldn't understand him. I often found myself trying to understand what he was telling me, and it wasn't until maybe after a year that I could really begin to understand.

One morning at the end of the Novices' Mass I saw Fr. Louis open the tabernacle and place an envelope, letter size, inside. He held it between his index finger and second finger and with his left hand placed it vertically inside the curtain. Then closed the door and finished Mass. I wasn't sure if that was a strange thing for a priest to do or not. Maybe there was some sort of blessing he wanted on this letter before he sent it.

Later that afternoon, or the day after, I went to the chapel for a visit. When I entered there was a flapping of wings as a bird flew from the altar out the front window on the left. I went to Fr. Tarcissius, the Undermaster, and told him a bird got into the chapel, and screens should be put on the windows. He said there are screens. I said, but not on the front two windows. When I went back, I saw they were sealed shut and never *were* opened.

At a conference following, Fr. Louis asked if anyone knew what became of the letter he had put in the tabernacle. No one answered.

It didn't seem right to me that anyone, at least not a novice, should be fooling around with the tabernacle unless he was Sacristan. And the Sacristan, Fr. David, had nothing to say.

A week or so later I passed the Undermaster's office and overheard something the two or three novices there were saying about "a miracle." I wasn't inclined to give attention to talk about miracles. I was grateful I hadn't heard much talk like that here yet. I supposed there was a lot of that sort of talk among the brother novices, and I was a little concerned it might be creeping over into the Choir Novitiate. So, I walked past the door without giving pause. Then at the next conference Fr. Louis said a woman he knew had been in a crisis. He read a letter from her that started out by saying: "I don't know how your letter, which was not postmarked, got here. I found it on the table when I walked into the house."

Then she expressed how it came at just the right time when she was in such darkness, etc. Fr. Louis didn't say how it got there either.

Later, in spiritual direction, when I tentatively brought up the letter in the tabernacle, Fr. Louis said we don't need to think about that too much. Christ can take care of these things.

He stimulated me more by example than by direct effort. There was only one time I remember when we did something artistic together. Somebody had brought a can of beer into his office and left it there. He invited me in, and we split the beer and drew pictures. After that he posted them up on the bulletin board and said, "There were two Russian artists here last night, Popov and Chekov."

I did write a poem when I was a novice and he liked it. He put it up on the board, and nothing much happened after that.

I didn't do a whole lot of writing until after he died. A person has to die before you inherit something of that spirit which moves them.

I sometimes made an effort to develop my imagination in the context of my spiritual life. That's one of Merton's chief qualities as a person, that he was a man of the imagination as well as the spirit. He was aware and awake and alive in his imagination and considered that to be an important part of his spiritual life. So, I've emulated that example. I would go around seeing things, angles, just the quality of light at certain times of the day, and how a certain configuration of space and objects can be very beautiful. But I didn't try to capture any of this until I started using a camera thirty years later.

He almost had to be out of the way before I could do it.[4] I couldn't feel my own space; I didn't feel I was somehow out from under his critical gaze until after he was gone. Then I was working from within, so to speak.

He would be more perceptive about me than I was about myself, and that would cause some tension. I never felt totally comfortable with him. He was a man with a gift of words and could use words quite pointedly, but he was also a man who was nonverbal in his ways of communication. He could penetrate through a smokescreen of words and leave you on the spot and knock you to another level of experience, where you had to cope with things without controlling them and rationalizing.

I remember one morning, within the first three months of my novitiate, when I went outside to the wall behind the novitiate, overlooking the valley. The sky was incredibly blue, and everything exquisitely fresh. My senses were cleansed by the rigor of our life and intensified by my budding manhood.[5] Everything in that quiet moment was more vivid than I ever knew before.

I strolled around the corner and Fr. Louis came by. He saw immediately into my soul and looked pleased. But when I saw that he saw, I was made self-conscious. He immediately saw that change come on and his look turned dark. This must have been a moment of what the Desert Fathers called "discernment of spirit." For me it was too much a moment of being obvious. So much happening without exchange of words was unsettling.

Another time, he was at work with the novices in the woods. I was standing a while worried over private things that a young man is likely to be worried about. He saw me, squeezed his eyes shut and burst out: "I'm never going to do that ever again"—as if reading my own thoughts. I was astonished. It startled me and broke the spell of the moment, but it didn't resolve my worry. Maybe I was becoming addicted to worry. And, moreover, I wasn't sure I wanted to be that easy to read.

I resist speaking about the following episode; perhaps it should be left alone and there is no business my putting it into words. But if I speak about Merton as I knew him, I might as well go all the way. The blocks against the nonverbal busted soon enough.

I had a dream, or something of the sort, since it started out with what seemed like a real shout from Fr. Louis's side room adjacent to the dormitory. I got up and ran to the socket in the wall and pulled out a plug. In reality there was no socket and no plug in that wall. I told Fr. Louis that dream the next day.

He said, "You saved my life." Then he told me he'd had a dream that he was electrocuted, he was lying on the floor in a room surrounded by monks and nuns and some big-wigs, and the Primate of the Benedictines was there. The coincidence of our dreams annoyed me and seemed pretty special. It never happened again.[6]

Fr. Louis spoke about the complaints that individuals make about our sermons in Chapter being so dull and windy. He said that the sermon a priest gives should be like a shout that a man standing outside a burning house makes to the people inside to get out. I was reluctant to pursue the thought of how he might apply that. Was it a shout to get out of the monastery that was as good as doomed? I was focused on trying to get in. Or did it speak to my own thought to get out of the Catholic Church, which sometimes seemed fatally constricted. Either interpretation was too narrow. His explanation used words such as "eschatological," "a different kind of world," and so forth. A shout to escape this world based upon illusion.

"Even a Zen monk has to forget his Zen sometimes," I heard him say once.

And, "The Lord made it known to me that if ever I abandon the hermitage I am finished." He said this at a Sunday conference, perhaps at the time he took a private vow as a hermit.

In spiritual direction, when I was talking about myself, or only thought I was, he said: "You are verbalizing." That stopped me and I felt exposed. I was still too distrustful and was covering up with words. I was maintaining a gap between my own view of myself and the view I presented to others. It was a pseudo-independence born of weakness.

He encouraged me to have more confidence in him: "I've had a lot of experience about our life in the monastery and I am here to help you." Things went better after that.

One day I came into the Grand Parlor, i.e., the changing room, where the toilets and showers are located, and found that the water was cut off and the toilets were not working. Soon, Fr. Louis walked in, and I told him the toilets were not working. With a sweep of the hand toward the field outside the window he said: "Hah, so what? The whole world is a toilet."

When it came to the question of what you prefer, dogs or cats, he said he preferred cats. "Dogs want to get your attention." He also was irritated about monks in the monastery who wanted a lot of attention.

I ran a telephone line to the hermitage so he could communicate with the monastery in case of an emergency. I said he could now talk to his friends. He raised his hands and threw them down and vehemently answered: "I don't want to have anything to do with any of them!"

That surprised me, since he had so many friends. The hermit was talking in him.

There were two separate dining rooms, one for infirm monks needing a meat diet, which was located next to the community refectory, where the rest of us took our meals. Readings for the meal came over loudspeakers in both rooms.

During one reading the lector came to a passage about the temptations of St. Jerome. The passage evidently read that Jerome imagined himself in a garden full of courtesans. But instead, the reader said: "in a garden full of Cartesians." One great hoot came from the next room.

Later, I asked Fr. Louis if that was him laughing, and he said it was Br. Fidelis. I asked Br. Fidelis and he said it was Fr. Louis.

During community chant practice for the feast of the Assumption, we were practicing the Introit, which starts with *Gaudiamus*. The last syllable "*mus*" is pronounced like moose. The Choir Director had us retry the sweeping melody and said, "Look out for the *mus*." Immediately Fr. Louis lifted his arms as if holding a rifle ready to shoot.

Fr. Louis celebrated an outdoor Mass with some nuns early one morning. When it came time at the Offertory to pour a drop of water into the wine chalice, he reached up, plucked a leaf from a tree and shook the dew drops into the chalice.

One of the neighbors of the monastery went rabbit hunting near Fr. Louis's hermitage. He spotted a rabbit in front of the porch and shot it. Fr. Louis came bursting out the door and yelled, "What are you doing shooting in front of my hermitage?"

The man said, "I'm hunting rabbits. I didn't tell him to stop there."

After some discussion, they became friends, and after that, the man would come visit sometimes.

The rest is rather paranormal, but this is how it was told to me: After Fr. Louis departed for Asia, the neighbor-hunter wandered up there and out the door came Fr. Louis. "I thought you were in Asia!" the man said. In reply, Fr. Louis said, "I am."

At the end of community dinner, the monks pour leftover coffee from their mugs and left-over scraps from their plates into a bucket. One day, someone threw the plate along with scraps into the full bucket. Fr. Louis was standing nearby, immediately pulled up the long sleeve of his cowl, and plunged his hand into the dirty water and retrieved the plate for him.

One time a young novice my age and I were reading in the empty Scriptorium. We got to making sign conversation through Trappist sign language. And as usual that was assisted by a few whispers. Fr. Louis came in. The Scriptorium was not supposed to be a place for conversations, so he told us to stop. Then he left, saying that he had to go see someone. After about fifteen minutes he came back and found us at the signs again. He said, "You will have to be more obedient than that if you want to stay in the monastery."

One novice who had entered the monastery after being in the seminary was having difficulty and decided to leave. Fr. Louis liked this novice and would confide some of his own complaints with him, which bothered the novice.

In preparation for the novice's departure, the two of them went to the Novitiate chapel and Fr. Louis gave him communion. When he received the host, Fr. Louis took his head and pressed it to the novice's chest. Later on in life the man became a diocesan priest.

An older novice who had been a lawyer caused amusement to Fr. Louis which he told me about. During spiritual direction when Fr. Louis was complaining about people in the monastery, the man stretched out his long legs and said, "Well, Father, to each his own." Fr. Louis liked that and repeated it often.

I was a rather agile young novice. There was a utility space above the asphalt tile ceiling in the novitiate. The access panel was next to Fr. Louis's office. I knew he was in there and I climbed a ladder and crawled through the upper space to the vent over his room. He heard someone coming and said, "Oh no!"

I said in a sweet tone: "This is your guardian angel."

He laughed.

I said, "I have something to tell you. You should give an extra dessert to Br. Paul in the refectory," all in the nicest manner.

He said, "You sound more like my aunt."

Decades later in his private journal, I read that he got a kick out of the younger novices.

Sometimes at conferences Fr. Louis would tell us about some visitor or other he had. After the Fellowship of Reconciliation retreat in 1964, which was attended by leading peace activists, he singled out one who was an elderly minister, a veteran at the peace work. What impressed him was a word he used in asking if he could write him a letter: "Would that be in accordance with your *covenant?*" That was A. J. Muste.[7]

During a conference on St. John of the Cross, Fr. Louis once said to us: "One thing about the dark night of the soul is you don't know if you will get through it."

Abba Barnabas was told once by Abba Louis, "I have reached the point in my spiritual life at which I am certain that I know nothing about the spiritual life."[8]

Abbot Timothy Kelly, OCSO

I was in the guest house for a week or so, which was normal when new people arrived for entry, and just washing dishes and living there. One evening the Guestmaster said, "The Novice Master will come to see you." I didn't know Thomas Merton was Novice Master. And so, this one evening the Guestmaster said, "Be in your room at 6:30, the Novice Master will come and see you." And so I was up there, and the Novice Master came and knocked on the door and introduced himself as the Novice Master and asked the usual questions a Novice Master would ask.

Since I'd been involved a little bit at the University of Toronto, he was interested in the Medieval Institute and the people there like Etienne Gilson.[9] He was asking me about that, and then he said, "Well, what do you know about the life?" And I said, "I've read all of Merton's published works and all of Fr. Raymond's published works and have a certain amount of historical awareness and so forth." And he said, "What do you think of the books?" And I said, "They're both rather romantic, although they have different perspectives." I said, "Certainly, Merton's style is much easier to handle than Raymond's." And he said, "Yeah, you really have to be careful what you read."

With that the interview ended.

The next morning the Guestmaster said, "Oh, did you see Thomas Merton, did you see Thomas Merton?" I said, "I saw the Novice Master." And he said, "Well, that's Thomas Merton."

"Oh-h-h."

He was a very enthusiastic teacher, a very excellent teacher. His conferences were always very well prepared, and often they were parts of some article he was writing. He called forth a lot of enthusiasm from his students. He would wax eloquently on some Latin father, and when you went to read it on your own, it just didn't quite have the same gripping interest.

He didn't want to gather disciples around him. He was always very objective in his teaching and if someone showed a bit of interest in his own person, who he was and so on, it was generally a sign that the person wasn't going to be around that much longer. It was just a part of his desire that he, Merton, not be attracting them to the monastic life but rather that the novices find their own basic monastic identity.

Barnabas Ahern[10] used to come to the community . . . and give these wonderful scriptural conferences, which were introducing us to modern scriptural exegesis. For Barnabas Ahern to stand up in the midst of this community and talk about whether the magi were historical figures or not was quite admirable in 1963–64. But with his own giftedness as a teacher and truly holy man that he was, he was quite able to pull it off.

In those conferences, at one time or another, he talked about Jonah as midrash. I'm quite sure most of us didn't understand what the term really meant. The next Sunday, Merton was giving the novices and juniors a conference based on the Scripture reading for the night office; we were reading the book of Jonah at the time. He waxed very eloquently in a poetic way about Jonah, who was a very special person in his own life. It is in *The Sign of Jonas* in "The Firewatch" where he talks about Jonah and the mercy upon mercy that is our gift.

One novice kept raising his hand, and finally,

he acknowledged him. He said, "Fr. Barnabas said Jonah's nothing but midrash." And with that, Merton closed his books, and he walked out and for a year or so never gave another Scripture conference. He said something to the effect that modern biblical scholars are ruining the culture of Christianity. I wouldn't say that's an exact quote, but it is something along that line.

He was always very generous with getting them [his famous writer and scholar friends] to give conferences to the novices or to the wider community, if it seemed proper. Also, I can remember when I was Undermaster, being aware of these very famous guests here to see him, and he'd be visiting with them. But when time came for him to see a brother for spiritual direction, he would leave and go to see him. He was always very conscious of his service to the community. He didn't use his notoriety as an escape from the day-to-day life of the monastery.

In those days the schedule was cut up into little sections, and he always was very disciplined and used every moment. He tried to inculcate this discipline into the life of novices. He encouraged us to know what we were going to do, what we were reading, what we were working with when the schedule gave us time; not to waste time, but to start immediately.

He was an excellent example of this. When it was time for reading, he would begin reading and read very assiduously, and when it was time to do something else, he did that very assiduously too. He would even say that in the old schedule, in the very truncated, cut-up schedule, he actually thought he got more work done than he did in the great empty periods in the hermitage, which I don't think is quite accurate. Even at the hermitage he was always a very disciplined worker.

[He was] always really alive! I wouldn't want to say exuberant, that would be too strong, but always "up." You really never experienced him as being down about something or negative. Always very positive, always very present to life, very present to the moment. Always seeing the humor of the present moment and also the pathos of it, and always very, very conscious and very alive to the place, to what he's doing and so on.

He was a scholar and a poet by temperament, yet one never really ran into him when he was preoccupied by other things. He was always really present. If you were speaking with him, he was very present to you. If he was doing something else, that's what he did. For example, because we eat in silence at some meals, brothers would bring a book to read at the meal. Fr. Louis would say, "Don't do that. When you eat, eat, and be present to what you're eating. Enjoy it, be aware of what you are eating. When finished eating, go do the reading."

One thing you'd say, Merton was always growing. That would be one of his weaknesses, even as a Novice Master. He didn't repeat himself. He was always having new visions or new ways of seeing things.

One Christmas time, on the feast of Thomas á Becket, when he read us great pieces of Eliot's drama *Murder in the Cathedral*, I can remember him getting very choked up with emotion and, in fact, ending the conference at that point where Becket speaks about the greatest treason is to do the right thing for the wrong reason. He did a little speech on that and he basically broke down, saying that this is one of the great dangers in life, one of the great trials in life.

That would be about the only time I really recall much personal show of emotion. He would often refer in a very general way to the fact that we all have things to do penance for, reasons why we struggle with life now because we made such a mess of it earlier or something like that. It wasn't a recurring theme, or at least I didn't pick it up as a recurring theme.

The day his death was announced to our community, it was announced in the refectory at the main meal. In those days, we used to get our mail put at our place in the refectory. There was an old monk; Fr. Alphonse was his name at that time. He had changed his name; it used to be Idesbald. He was Belgian by birth and had come to this country in 1917 or so, right after the First World War, and never really learned English. He was only in the country for about a year when he joined the community here. So as an old man, he really didn't have a language. He'd forgotten his Flemish, if anyone could speak Flemish here, and he never really did learn English, and he didn't know that much French. He was a person who had certainly a lot of frustration in his life. I guess nowadays you'd put it in terms of anger. But a real character in the community. Always a bit marginal, but just a "character." It is the only word I can use, a good person but someone to whom you didn't pay that much attention.

So the day Merton died, it was announced

in the refectory. Fr. Alphonse comes up to me with a postcard in his hand trying to understand it. He said, "You know, they said he died, but I just got this postcard from Fr. Louis." And I thought, "Wow!" It was true. He had a postcard sent from Thailand just saying, "Hi, how are you? I hope it was not too much work with cheese and fruitcake this year, and I'm going to be with the monks in Hong Kong for Christmas," and ended up by saying, "Behave yourself now," or something like that. Here is Merton over meeting the Dalai Lama and doing all these things he wanted to do, and he sent this postcard to this old man. . . . I always think that was the true Merton. Very much aware of people in the community and especially the marginal people, and very willing to acknowledge their presence in just a simple show of friendship.

When I first came to Gethsemani, what we picked up as a spirituality would have had a very strong emphasis on doing a lot of *things*, pious acts, extra penance, obviously fulfilling the obligations. It was just *doing* a lot. He would not encourage this, although he was always very disciplined and always very respectful of the structures.

Rather, he would speak of it in other terms. He would remind us that we weren't just doing such things because they were penitential or doing these things because they curbed our self-will or something. He would speak of it more in terms of freedom. You did these things in order to become free from those other elements in your life that held you back or that confused you, or whatever it is. He subtly put a different emphasis on a lot of monastic practices, which made them much more realizable, or much more positive than just something done as an exercise. They were really for growth and for knowing yourself.

I always use the "true self" and that type of vocabulary—which was an underlying theme in all his teachings—to help a person come to know really what it is that he wants to do with his life, how it is that he best can live the gospel. Merton was always encouraging novices to come really to that understanding rather than accepting a form of life because it supposedly is perfect and supposedly is very good. No, no! Finding what it is, where you can use your talents, or you can be yourself most honestly, is the essential.

He was always very supportive and encouraged people to find their way. There was here [at the Abbey of Gethsemani], very much [at that time], the axiom that you were saved while you were here, but if you got off Noah's Ark [so to speak], the devil's right at the front door there waiting to attack you as soon as you walk out the door. Merton did not agree with that at all.

Everybody's always trying to make him into some type of a myth. I wonder if his voluminous writing isn't part of his own effort to keep from becoming a myth. . . . Because, if you read it all, there's a lot for edification, but there's also a way that one recognizes a very human, in the best sense of the word, person.

It's interesting how brutally honest he is in writing about his own life. I think in some sense it makes him a much more acceptable person or model because one can find in him a lot of one's own reality—I wouldn't say struggles, but his own difficulties, something to relate to and something to find hope for. If this man could hold together such divergent and disparate views and bring them together, bring them to some type of resolution, then we too are hopeful for spiritual integration.

Father Chrysogonus Waddell, OCSO

I don't think anyone here in the monastery was all that particularly close to him, at least among those who have stayed. He was a private person in most of his community contact and didn't invite much by way of personal intimacy. I think there were some to whom he felt more sympathetic, people like Ernesto Cardenal or Fr. John of the Cross, who you would almost think got sometimes emotionally dependent. But, in general, I think he was a man who was tremendously solitary, and he could show various aspects of himself having to do with people according to the circumstances. I think you would be a little bit puzzled if there was anyone in the community who would say that they had an especially close relationship, apart, maybe, from Dom James or someone who really had pretty immediate, direct contact with him over a long period of time.[11]

When I first came, they had the Office of Our Lady every day, the Office of the Dead every day, plus the solemn Canonical Office. And we had a heavy work schedule. There was very, very, little time. So, for several years before that, I think Fr. Louis was much concerned about reducing, you might say, the quantity of liturgical prayer, for the sake of what he thought should be more serious prayer—to get the Office over quickly, and then you would have more time for your serious prayer in solitude. I can understand that absolutely perfectly.

Gradually it was realized—I forget what the dates were . . . 1956, something like that—when the Little Office of Our Lady was dropped, the Office of the Dead was reduced to just once a month. So, we did have a little bit more air in which to breathe.

At that time everything was in Latin and Gregorian chant. Now there was no one who loved to chant, and the Latin, more than Fr. Louis. And I think that development paradoxical. I suppose you know his fine takeoff on Rahner's study of the Christian Diaspora?[12] It's been a long time since I read Fr. Louis's article but, as I remember, he more or less argued that the time is going to come when we were going to have real monks in an urban setting, maybe over a tavern or a beer garden or something. But you have to be careful not to throw out the really important things, like the chant, the Latin, the traditional texts—Latin Gregorian chant.

And so he had passionate love for the liturgy, especially for the interiorization of the liturgy. For him, that was the almost essential item. That nevertheless raised enormous problems for a lot of people in the community. Newcomers, upon experiencing difficulties in achieving the goal of "contemplative prayer," would feel frustrated in their efforts to push the right button so as to produce the desired effect—instant contemplation. Or, again, the monk who did experience a kind of spiritual "high" or peak experience would try to prolong it by some kind of unrealistic psychological effort. When this didn't work, the tendency was to blame it on the liturgy. And I think when it came to Fr. Louis, throughout his whole life, there was an intellectual dichotomy.

I don't think that was ever resolved in a really significant way. But I think at the level of experience, it was quite, quite the opposite. His actual experience was positive. He always celebrated the Office in Latin. I remember when I told him, a year or two before his death that Prime was no longer obligatory in the [Trappist] Order, so we didn't have to say Prime unless he wanted to, and he said, "Chrysogonus, Prime is a problem for you cenobites, not for us hermits." And so he always prayed his Office. Sometimes when he was outside the monastery, other monks were a little broader in interpretation of the obligation to the Office, and were a little taken aback: [there was] Fr. Louis, the *avante garde*, appearing in an activist life, but still hauling out his Breviary in order to say Vespers at awkward times of day.

I remember once he was playing a recording—I think it was the *Goldberg Variations* [of Johann Sabastian Bach] to the novices—and Brother Killian who was in charge of everything electronic walked into the room and Fr. Louis had all the adjustments completely the opposite of what was supposed to be. That never phased him the least bit! He wasn't sensitive to that aspect. He heard the voice line, or he heard the substance of the music. But just the sheer sound, the tone quality, the mere acoustical quality of it just didn't make that much of an impression on him. And a lot of people I know who are electronic experts hear nothing but the pure physical sound of it.

He was a tremendously changeable person. He reflected a great deal into the way he comported himself. I think many of the brethren thought he was very excitable. I remember one of them used the term "French babbler," which is a technical expression. But at times he would, like myself, wave his arms around and use his whole body. At other times, he could quite consciously just be physically totally recollected. I think it took an effort of will.

If, for example, the Abbot came over to speak with the novices, then Fr. Louis, in the Abbot's presence, would simply fade into the background. It was a little bit unnatural because I think most of the time it was more normal for him in a given situation not to dominate it but to be at the center, and maybe bring out the best of other people participating. But with an authority figure, he would quite consciously just withdraw. And you see him, for example, in photographs occasionally taken of the community celebrating the liturgy. You'll find Fr. Louis there in the deepest recollection. It's just something almost—something metaphysical.

And so I think that was part of his technique.

I know he used to practice yoga during one particular period, and then he had difficulty with his back and sort of turned to Zen. So, I think that was quite serious. And I think he was worried about putting on too much weight toward the end of his life. I remember once he remarked to me that he hoped it wasn't compulsive eating. It was more than just a joke.

I remember once I got him a little bit irritated. He was telling me about how he went about his writing in the afternoon. He would go off for a couple of hours to St. Anne's field, and sit under what used to be a little sort of shed with a bell. It's no longer there. Or he'd sit on the ground, and toward the end of the afternoon what he had written would come to about ten pages of paper.

And then I made some kind of vague comment about maybe it would be good to go over the material more carefully and the immediate response was, "But I'm a very careful writer!"

He took it as a real criticism, and I suppose it was. I really hadn't meant it. I was not in any position to criticize Fr. Louis as a writer. Although I guess I felt sometimes it would maybe be better to have sat on a few ideas a bit longer and work out things a little more carefully.

So, I think he was a tremendously intuitive person and usually the first draft was splendid and really would pass muster. He really didn't have to do that much rewriting all the time.

But I think he might have felt a little bit guilty about that, at times. . . . I think actually a lot of the time he spent in quiet prayer, in solitude, actually part of that was just for his thinking of life, organizing ideas, getting involved with his subject.

I used to get a little irritated at some of his "anti-poems" and I thought he could be just a little glib.[13] I remember making once a remark that he didn't like too much. He was speaking with a group of the community about his "anti-poems" and reading out loud; he began by saying that this isn't supposed to "mean" anything. You're not supposed to look for any meaning in it! And then he started reading these "anti-poems" which I find are tremendously exciting; and then he started asking the question, "What did you get out of it?" And they got quite irritated. Some of the brethren obviously answered, "I haven't gotten anything out of it." And then I asked the question, "Were we *supposed* to get something out of it?"

I think he was the kind of person who was at his best when he was doing a lot of things that seemed apparently incompatible with the way he had analyzed his own vocation at an earlier stage. I remember he was all the time making statements in which he was very defensive about anyone trying to categorize him. So, he didn't claim to be a hermit, monk, you know, in a certain sense. And he didn't claim to be anything. He just had his own personal unique vocation.

Fr. Louis's main villain was Fr. Louis. And then again, he always integrated something within a deeper experience, and it wasn't a question of his leaving one thing for another thing, but I think his maybe reaching out and integrating something within that may be deeper.

My own impression is that it wasn't a question of "leaving behind," but of integrating his past in a new, more vital and broader synthesis. More a question of integration than of rejection.

I think he was really writing very much for people who weren't specifically Christian. . . .

So, when he's talking about contemplation and spiritual liberation and freedom, that is exactly the point, but I think the deepest reality for him was the mystery of Christ.

Christ was the center of Fr. Louis's experience, even when he couldn't or wouldn't be explicit about this—often because of the persons to whom he was addressing himself. I think he thought it was something of a rupture, or an area of difficulty between the truth and those to whom he was addressing. And I think also there is a real humble streak there, not a streak of pride, but a streak of real humility.

In his better moments he was really serious about wanting to learn from other people and so that he would maybe avoid areas where there would be fundamental differences and was really trying to elicit what the other person could share with him that would mean a real communion.

I think his real need was to feel sat on, and to feel a little bit persecuted. He wasn't comfortable, I think, with being just accepted. He needed desperately to be a real prophet, and a prophet just can't be understood. So, I think when people understood him, he was afraid of being understood by the Establishment. Then he would react desperately against that.

I remember once he was making his thanksgiving after Communion in a little storage room in the rear of the old Sacristy, and the Sacristan just opened the door to look for something and he turned on the lights while Fr. Louis was there and flipped off the lights and left. But that afternoon we got a conference in the Juniorate[14] about the type of monastic personality who goes around snooping into other people's lives and trying to turn the lights on their interior lives.

I knew exactly—I was in the Sacristy at the time—what triggered that off.

But I also know old Fr. Cletus. He just had to get something from the room, and he didn't realize Fr. Louis was back there. So, all the time, Fr. Louis was experiencing things in a poetic, symbolic way and I think his response was just marvelous. I think the thing that he says very often as a result of that type of experience is meaningful, but I would never reconstruct the historic situation on the basis of the way Fr. Louis described it!

Fr. Louis, I remember, just before he became Novice Master, had a couple of us who were helping him move his books to the other side of the monastery. He paused at the end of the afternoon and said, "This is the last time I will ever be speaking to you as your Father Master, so what's the most important thing I have to say?" He said that the monk is the man who truly seeks God, and the emphasis has to be on the word "truly" because you just can't seek God.

A lot of people are doing that in a kind of funny way. You have to seek God truly, there where he has revealed himself most perfectly—in Christ. And I think Fr. Louis was all the time seeking God truly. He said at that time—I never will forget it—that the moment you think you've found God all that perfectly, in that moment you've really stopped seeking God, and you've lost him.

Father John Eudes Bamberger, OCSO

I was there for quite some time before I knew which one was Merton. I discovered that one day when we had a class and he was teaching it. That was some weeks, and maybe even a month or two, after I entered.

But I do recall that he wasn't the one I would have picked out as being Merton. If you read about someone you sort of guess who it would be, but he would have been about the last one I would have guessed.

There was a kind of elegance about his mind and style, I felt, and a kind of clarity and forcefulness, and so looking for someone to match that wasn't the way to identify Merton. He didn't come across that way at all as an actual presence.

Merton was a very warm, and basically a very sympathetic person, who had gone deeply into his own experiences, and who had been in touch with a wide range of his emotions and inner experiences that related to culture, art, and so on. He was a communicator. So that when he spoke about things, he spoke in a concrete way, and you felt you were talking to somebody who wasn't just repeating something he had read.

Also, he spoke with warmth and conviction, and even enthusiasm, and finally with a certain sense of intimacy that you felt as you read his books. I think people still feel that way.

What he said in the preface to the Japanese edition of *The Seven Storey Mountain*—if you read this book and listen attentively, maybe you'll hear the same person whom I hear when I write it—I think that that is just what he conveyed. He took you with him into the presence of God, communing with His Spirit.

The Seven Storey Mountain—he talked to me about that one day.

He said, "Really it's a bad book in many ways, and people complain about it. It really needs to be rewritten, but it's not mine anymore."

I never felt that way. I still think it's his best book, and it always will be because it's the truest. It's got all kinds of exaggerated opinions. It's not balanced or anything, but who cares about that? It's the way it was. It's the slice of life the way he lived it. And that's what literature is, and it's the way God works with people.

I think so many people had false notions of him. When he said things about Dom James, he exaggerated, and they weren't true in that way, but when you knew him, they were.

He deals in metaphor, and also you have this particular artist with his very, very sensitive reactions, spontaneous reactions, who is convinced that in the end, if you let it all come out, the truth will be available, and those who have good will and enough sensitivity will see it.

Who cares what the others think anyhow? To me, that's the way he looked at it.

I think what he aimed at chiefly, when he taught us, was the right spirit: that the thing to emphasize is being personally committed to the Lord, living from the heart, being a genuine person. He felt very strongly about that.

And in his relations with people, if he ever thought you were not operating that way, he would get very abrupt with you. And that was the chief thing. But then, I believe, many of the changes in our [religious] order favor that, and were made specifically with that in mind, with facilitating a more personal involvement.

His writings antedate Vatican II quite a bit, you know, like *The New Man* and *No Man Is an Island*, and so on. His writings already were inculcating this. When he taught a Scripture course back in 1952 and '53, he was stressing essentially these points: resurrection, freedom, personal engagement with the Risen Lord, and so on. And I felt that was the essence of his message. That also got into Vatican II. He was just ahead of it, that's all.

There was a streak in him of a pure kind of humility that I never quite understood. For example, he would take advice from a confessor, see, who was not very intelligent or very cultivated, and he took it very seriously, because he felt that the confessor spoke in God's place.

I remember when I was a young monk there—I forget what the question was—but he asked me a question concerning something in his own life. I started telling him what I thought about it, and I could tell that he was taking my answer very seriously in the sense of really looking for some guidance for himself, in a way you wouldn't expect of your Father Master, see?

I don't think he ever lost that. It relates to his gift of faith, and also to a kind of simplicity. Although he was very intelligent and very quick, his temperament and his intelligence didn't dominate. I think his writing was that type of thing, too. It was there. It would compete at times, but when he stood back and looked at things, something else was always more important.

Father Matthew Kelty, OCSO

The church was dark and gloomy, not depressing, but dark, the whole house was dark, being even dirty compared to now. The church wasn't painted. It hadn't seen paint for God knows how long. That was deliberate because the monks knew some day they were going to redo it anyhow, and it would have wasted money to make an effort in that direction. Anyway, I came in 1960, it was November, dark and gloomy, and I saw Fr. Andrew who was the Guestmaster and I was there three or four days and then I wanted to enter.

The first one to receive me was Fr. John Eudes Bamberger who was the psychiatrist. And he didn't give you much attention. He just asked a few, almost *blasé*, questions, nothing very striking. I didn't think they were very telling. He just said they get a lot of priests coming here who were just coming to get away from their orders or societies. . . . And then Merton came along and just asked a few simple questions. It was not very astonishing.

And that's all. And both of them were about as indifferent as if they couldn't care less. That was deliberate; I realized that after a while. They probably, even today, do that. They don't entice you, and beg you, or cajole you or make any effort at all to coax you to enter or something like that. It's up to you. If you want to try it . . . that's about as much interest as they showed. The Abbot, Dom James Fox, was a little more positive. And that was the first meeting. And then when I came, I came in January or February 1960, then Merton was Novice Master.

He didn't think of himself as famous, or interesting, or a character, or a well-known writer. He simply didn't take himself that seriously; and when you don't, nobody else will. They will react to you the way you react to yourself. And they took him very casually. They treated him just like any other monk. And we would hear very little about his impact on the literary world in any case.

The books, when they did appear, were up in the library on the table and nothing special would be made of them. I don't remember any of his books being read in refectory, but they did read one or two, I think, before my time. There was no big announcement made. We had no idea, in fact, that he was well known.

We had no idea that Merton's impact was as great as it was. It was a bombshell to most of us to find out how great a man he was.

Occasionally he would share guests with us; you know, get them to talk to the novices. The Abbot would let him.

The Berrigans did, once or twice.

Then we had Evans. He was a Dominican. Illtud Evans.[15] He was editor of *Blackfriars*. He talked to us one day. I remember him particularly. He's very British. He's learned . . . a Dominican, you know, a very learned man, the kind of man that Merton loved, and he had toured the States and he came especially to see some of the abbeys. He visited Collegeville and then there was a friary in St. Louis, built in very modern style; then there was another one out in Rhode Island someplace. These were a little bit advanced in their style. He was praising them, and I could remember, we novices didn't go along with him. We told him we didn't like these new monasteries, these great German masses of concrete. We thought it was hideous. And we said we thought that the National Shrine of the Immaculate Conception, which was just being finished in Washington, was much more typical of the United States.

He didn't comment on Gethsemani, but he was proud of the fact the monastic orders had the most advanced architecture. We said we didn't agree with that. I mean we weren't saying the Shrine of the Immaculate Conception was all that great, but it was typical of the American Catholic viewpoint, and the American bishops, that it would be much more representative of the Catholic Church than St. John's in Collegeville would be. St. John's would be for an elite, a very small group.

But . . . Merton would take it very much amiss if you criticized his guests or disagreed with them or spoke out, didn't treat them with great civility. We weren't uncivil to Evans. But I didn't realize that Merton would get very annoyed. Finally, Dom James told me, "Don't do that, don't pick on his guests."

Well, we had a very quiet life. We saw nobody, and we were restricted here in this confine, then much more than now, and we were all new at it, we had just come. You move into an environment where all outside stimulus is cut off, there's no input. It's to awaken the inner life. So, there's nothing coming in from outside. But all of his friends were intellectually stimulating, original thinkers, and many of them were professional. They were speakers, lecturers, and they deliberately set out to antagonize you, to stimulate you by making extraordinary statements. These people would come into us novices and in no more than ten minutes, we'd be jumping out of the chairs. He'd get very annoyed.

He thought of himself, I'm sure he did, as physically capable, but I thought he was dangerous with an axe. He thought of himself as not exactly athletic, for he talked about his failure as a rower with the boats. He wasn't all that coordinated. He wasn't handy. Let's put it that way. He wasn't handy with stuff, tools, and things.

I remember one day we were all coming in from work or something. It was the afternoon, around three or something, and there was an enormous black cloud of smoke up there on the hill. It would have been right in the dry time, in the fall sometime. Fires can be very dangerous here. And so he rounded us all up and we all went just as we were, robes and all, we went gallivanting up the hill, and he took charge. And he wouldn't let us run; he made us walk fast. And we all had brooms; there was a fire broom each of us took along. And the whole woods was a roaring fire because one of the neighbors was burning something in the back of his yard and it had gotten out of hand.

And, of course, his hermitage was right in the middle of all that. But I never forgot it because he was showing more than just ordinary concern, telling us, "All right, men, now, go here, now we'll do this," shouting orders. We got it out, though.

It was so unlike him. It was so out of context, as the military leader leading this expedition to put out this fire.

He would frequently bitch about the Abbot and we always understood this to mean that, you know, he criticized the Abbot. He'd find fault with him, the Abbot did this or that. . . . And we novices, we understood this perfectly.

The idea was that the Abbot is a human being. He is the head of this monastery. You take vows to God Almighty through the hands of this Abbot. If you cannot live with his imperfections and human frailty, well, don't get involved then. If your faith isn't deep enough to go beyond this, you're simply out of your element. In other words, he wasn't out to put the Abbot up as some glorified figure, the Christ figure, whom you would find it easy to obey. You took your vows to God through this man, and this man was a human being, and he wouldn't pull any punches. He would tell us what this old man's job was, what this man was up to. So, it was done frankly but without this sneering backbiting sort of thing. Very objective.

He told me himself that he was an artist, a poet. He was a romantic, he was a dreamer, he had a new idea every week, and he would get all worked up over these ideas, and then he would go running off to the Abbot with them, and the Abbot would sit and listen to him patiently and, of course, eventually tell him the whole thing was just a dream. Then he'd bitch a bit and then go back where he was and start over again. And he told me himself that Dom James was the kind of Abbot that he needed. If he had had a soft-hearted, easy, benevolent Abbot, he would have ended up a disaster. His gifts were so strong and so wild that he needed this control if they were going to amount to anything. And he told me that himself.

The monks used to think he was kind of a wild one, you know, that he got away with a great deal. And he would give you this impression, you know, because he was not out to create a following. He hated that. He did not want a cult; he was vehement on this.

He'd get wild if he thought people were cultivating him, you know, or were making a fetish out of him. But Dom James himself told me that he had no more obedient monk than Merton. He would bitch and make a lot of noise about something, but when it came to a showdown, he'd obey. And the Abbot knew this. This is why the Abbot could give him a great deal of rope, because he could trust him. But in the end, if he said "No" it was finished. He'd give him a real good talking to, and the matter was settled.

And those were the principles Fr. Louis taught us. Being a good, obedient monk didn't mean that you lived forever in a kind of equanimity with your Abbot on every single issue. There were many areas where you could be in disagreement, and even in contention if you thought it was serious enough; but in the end the decision was the Abbot's, and that's the way the life is set up. And he lived up to it.

I think in the Abbey, [the impact our ways had upon the natural environment] was probably the thing that he made the biggest stink about, and with certain departments, you know, that would be the Cellarer, Brother Clement, who was in charge of the farm and who was a modern farmer, and who did everything just like right out of a book.

I never saw a farm like the one we had. I came from a different [religious] order and at our seminary we had a farm. We were in some ways more of a monastery than this place was. We grew our wheat and made our own flour and baked our own bread. The equipment was old hand-me-downs and poor stuff and you had to fix it up, you know. I mean it was antiquated. And this place was modern, up to date, and that meant going along with all that involved—pesticides, for instance, to make the crops grow because our land is not that good. And then they watered all these fields with these irrigation pipes, you know, and lakes they made . . . because it gets dry here. It doesn't rain maybe for a month or so. And then it all had to be sprayed with pesticides. And Merton would go wild over this, because it would kill everything, bugs and birds, bees and butterflies, in order to make this alfalfa. You know our alfalfa would be up to your waist and the neighbors' would be like clover around your ankles.

Then . . . there was a creek that wandered through the fields . . . and it was more fertile ground because it's lowland, but the creek wandering through it made it very difficult to cultivate it, and so they moved the creek, put it over on the further side.

Well, that went on, I think, for months, day and night, or at least they worked in the moonlight, you know. They moved that creek over to the one side so that they could, you know, do the corn or whatever it was in one clean sweep.

He bitched about that without end, because he couldn't sleep at night. He'd write nasty notes. . . . He didn't like the idea of tearing up this creek.

Later on, the water returned. But bulldozers, pawing through, tearing up woods and spreading chemicals. This sort of thing annoyed him to no end.

The [Daily] Office was longer and complicated, feast days were apt to be very elaborate with very long Offices. Whenever they would do anything, they'd tend to make it big.

He was very low key. I remember the class a year ahead of me, before I came. They took one little room off of the office in the Novitiate, before Christmas, and tore everything out and then built a crib, a big Christmas scene inside. He was very annoyed. Because they wasted valuable time. Just because of Christmas, because the room was for Christmas, you don't have to make work out of it. Oh, he'd get very, very nasty.

He didn't mind a little decoration, but all that running out to the woods and bringing in all kinds of green, spending all day working on it. And then they used to have a Corpus Christi procession in the cloister. You've seen pictures of it in Europe? This got more and more elaborate every year that I was here because you'd have to go out and gather all these flowers, and because there weren't enough flowers, they'd go out and gather greens, and grind them up in one of the farm machines, so you could handle them. You'd get different colored kinds of grass and gravel. The whole cloister floor was covered with this carpet of flowers and greens in designs.

After he was living up there [in his hermitage] a while, it got to be known where he was, and priests from the area used to come. They knew that you could park on the highway up there and cut across the fields, and then climb over the fence to the woods. And it got to be so bad that, in the end, in the afternoons, you'd find him out in the woods because people would come to him. But he told me, too, that priests, like in Louisville, which is what we were talking about, "If they need me, I would gladly spend myself for them. I would give up my solitude." What he resented was people coming to him just like they were tourists or something. If people had problems and worries or wanted somebody to talk to, he would be very glad to see them. He never would turn them away.

I don't know much about intellectuals. I sometimes get the impression that intellectuals love stimulating dialogue, and he could do this. He could be very exciting in his talks, lectures, and so on, and say really outrageous things and then come back tomorrow and, without batting an eye, contradict everything he said yesterday. Without, you know, thinking that there's any reason to apologize, because he's seeing it today from this side, and yesterday he was seeing it from that side. And it was up to you to figure it out.

In this context, in this life, too much excitement is not good for you, too much emotion, too much, you know. And he used to get me excited, even annoyed, get me all worked up. Reading him is different, but hearing him . . .

The Brothers[16] used to go down and cut up the vegetables for dinner, early in the morning, four o'clock or something . . . and they resented it as time went on, and when the new look began to come into the life, they wanted more time for reading. A lot of this was make-do work, wasn't really necessary . . . sometimes it was, but sometimes it wasn't. And so they began to fall off; they figured let the cooks do it themselves.

And then we had an eager beaver, a young father, appointed to be Master of the Brothers, and he was wanting to get all the Brothers down there in the morning, because those who went resented the fact that others didn't come, you know, the usual community thing. And in order to entice the Brothers to come to work, he would tape Merton's conferences to the Novices today at eleven o'clock and would play it the next day at four o'clock in the morning, because in those days, there was no contact between the different departments.

Merton might just as well have been any-where as far as they were concerned, because they never heard him talk. At most maybe once a year, in a Chapter talk, and you couldn't go to confession to him. You weren't allowed to speak to him, seeing him occasionally, that's all. And they had no awareness of his spiritual teaching because it wasn't yet available.

And so one day we went to a conference at 11:15, I think it was, and there was a microphone hanging in front of him. He said, "Today we're on the air." And I said, "Who's listening to you?" "Well," he said, "the Brothers will." I said, "How are the Brothers listening to you, because there's nobody in the house." He said, "The Brothers down in the workroom." I said, "They're not down in the workroom now." He said, "It's on tape. It's going to be put on tape."

Tape was fairly new then; tape recorders weren't everywhere. Well, I thought, for Heaven's sake! And we were surprised that he went along with it, because he didn't have much sympathy for electronic business. So, then they started and all the Brothers flocked to the workroom. They went, because it was the first time they had heard him. Well, that started them to work. It was a trick to get them there. And then from then on, they recorded all of his conferences, and then they were better in the original because . . . the originals were better than the printed form because his talks were always preceded by his little . . . small talk around the abbey, little jokes, and then questions from the audience and that sort of thing. And then they went on further, and began to record any address that he made, and by the time he died, they had a whole cabinet full.

It was Gerard Majella, that's the Father's name. He's gone now. He left. He was the Father Master for the Brothers. It was his idea.

I would always think of him not as being brilliant and an intellectual and all that. I think of him as being poor, and simple, and little, and fragile, and dearly loved.

I'm not an intellectual, so I don't understand all that. People think of him as brilliant and all this, but he thought of himself as a poor sinner whom God infinitely loved. He reflected this in his whole manner and that's the way he affected people.

He did not impress you. He was not an impressive person. He was not an impressive figure, even his face was plain. This isn't to criticize other people, some people exhibit power and strength, but he didn't. And his lesson was how good God is, how sweet God is, and how loving God is, even for the littlest and poorest and the most fragile of us. Do you follow me?

His last appearance among us was in that monstrous casket in our sanctuary while we did our last service to him. He was Jonah in the belly of the whale. He was the man totally committed to the mercy of God, about to be cast on the eternal shores. Mercy was his other name.

Father Flavian Burns, OCSO

You know, he was an artist with words both in writing and in speaking. This was true even in ordinary conversation.

He was very lively in his speech. Sometimes I wasn't always happy with his sense of humor because I felt a little bit that he used it to keep you at a certain distance. A lot of people do that—especially I think the English and the Irish—people that keep you at a certain distance by humor. But for the most part, it was pleasant and enjoyable.

And he couldn't sit still, you know. The monastery is rather a serious place, and you have a lot of reading in public and a lot of speaking in public and there's a lot of things going on and most of the monks keep their eyes down; don't let on what's going on. He wasn't like that. He'd let on. He'd comment on everything, if it was only by eye movements, a surprised look, something like that.

Even his script was abrupt. He didn't hesitate. Like if he typed things up, he might go over it and correct some things. Most of us, if we write a letter, we'd think about it and we'd weigh which phrase to use. I don't think he did that. He did these things like that [snaps fingers]. And if he didn't like it, maybe he would throw it away, but usually he'd let things stand.

And he wrote his journal notes in a ledger . . . precisely, I think, so that he couldn't be pulling pages out and throwing them away. And if he was going to correct something that he said or take it back or anything like that, well, he'd do it on the next page . . . so that the shifting opinions or thoughts would be all there. He seemed to have the honesty of doing this journal business.

I remember when I was a young monk asking him about the advisability of my keeping a journal. And he said, "Oh, I wouldn't do that."

I said, "Well, why not?" He said, "You'd waste too much time."

And I said, "Well, you keep a journal."

He said, "Yeah, but I write real fast."

And I think it was exactly true. I didn't appreciate it at the moment, but, on reflection, I accept it as being very accurate.

I remember one time we had a council meeting discussion when he was Father Master of Novices. I was Prior and there was a complaint on the part of one of the other members of the council that he, Merton, wasn't around when the novices needed him. He answered that by saying that he saw each of the novices—and there were quite a number at that time—once a week or whatever the time period was. He didn't think it was right for him to be sitting there so they could run in to him whenever they had any little problem.

He said, "We're training these people to be able to live the solitary life to some extent . . . life alone with God. We'd better find out in the first couple of years that they are here whether they can do that or not."

So even if he seemed impatient, I think he was actually a very patient man. He was certainly patient with me.

I think he was not willing to accept falsehood or people wanting to talk when there was no reason for it and things like that.

He used to tease us occasionally about things that we would do, for example, in passing one another. We were supposed to be living in silence. There was a prescribed little bow that you made so you didn't act like you weren't there. But usually the American outgoing manner, or self-consciousness—which was more or less what he was telling us it was—would engage us, and we would have to make some joke or passing remark.

I remember one time he was telling us that we didn't really believe in silence if we felt it was necessary to do that. One should be able to pass somebody in silence.

He didn't see too many outsiders. But he was the type that, if somebody came, he would give that person everything he had, all of his time, all of his energy. Well, naturally, when he returned to his quietude, he'd feel that.

So, it was important for him, I think, to have a lot of physical solitude because otherwise he would just run himself out. I'm not built like that, and I can handle a little more of it.

And so, the only way you could really keep him to himself was to protect him to some extent from himself. A lot of the people who complained about the old[17] Abbot [Dom James Fox] and all that are not being very realistic to the providence that God had in mind. And even Fr. Louis realized that if he hadn't had that he could have used himself up very easily on superficial things. And this is why, even when I was Abbot, my aim was to get him a more private place because I knew that if he had more physical solitude, he would use it well. But if he was going to be where people could get at him, he was going to respond to that.

He spent his time well. If you go over his schedules in the hermitage, for example, another writer might get up in the middle of the night and write books and things like that, but he spent his time well, frequently in prayer. He spent his time walking in the woods.

I remember going to speak with him following the first time I myself walked in the woods with him and the group of Scholastics. He asked how I liked it. I said, "Well, it was all right but by the time we got out there and I got settled I didn't get much reading in." And he sort of looked at me with mock horror and said, "Reading? You brought a book?" The time was so scarce in those days, and we had so much that we were supposed to read and study that the thought of just going out and wasting a whole afternoon walking through the woods was something that we found a little hard to do.

There were certain times of the day when he would say you should never touch a book, before such and such a time, or this, or that. I think most people felt that they had to use their time "well." They didn't have the idea of "holy leisure" that he had.

I owe him more than I owe any other human being, I think, for what I really treasure in my life. I don't see how I could have gotten the insights into various things without his help. So, I haven't a bad thing to say about him.

I think he reveals himself more in his writings than he did face to face. Because I think on a face-to-face personal level, he kept a distance. He had to relate to them differently. But he was very protective, very modest; whereas in his writings, I sensed, that this man is talking from his heart. And it's all laid out there. I think that's what people pick up.

Maybe that's what made him so protective. He knew himself that he was "doing it." Naturally you read something, and you're touched, and then you want to sit down and talk to the man. You feel you're going to get right on that level with him. Well, you can't. He wasn't up to doing that with complete strangers, whereas he could do it in his books.

Glossary of Monastic Words and Phrases

Breviary: a religious book containing the prayers and services for each day, as used in Roman Catholic religious orders.

Chapter: a regular meeting of the members of a religious house.

Compline: prayer service at night, said, chanted, or sung before departing for bed.

Daily Office: the regular, daily, liturgical hours of communal prayer in a monastery.

Desert Fathers and Mothers: early Christian hermits (third and fourth centuries) in Egypt and Syria, known for their wisdom and aphoristic teachings.

Guestmaster: the monk who is responsible for welcoming guests from the outside and finding them suitable accommodations.

Hermitage: the dwelling of hermit, or solitary, which is usually remote, simple, and small.

Novice Master (or Master of Novices): the monk of a monastery with primary responsibility for teaching and training the Novitiate.

Novitiate: both the period of time during which a monk remains a novice, and the place in the monastery that houses all of the novices.

Primate: the title for a bishop who has authority over other bishops.

Prior: the monk who is one step below the Abbot in authority in the monastery.

Scholastics: those monks who are studying, between the Novitiate and their ordination to the priesthood.

Sacristan: the monk in charge of the Sacristy, the space in the church that houses the priestly vestments and various instruments needed for worship.

Tabernacle: a fixed, secure box in a Catholic Church used for holding the Eucharist (consecrated communion hosts) in reserve.

Undermaster: the monk assigned to assist a Master (of Novices, of Brothers, etc.).

Vespers: evening prayer in the monastery, said, chanted, or sung.

Further Reading

To get a deeper glimpse into Thomas Merton's life, in every respect, the best place to go is into his journals that were published beginning twenty-five years after his death. These are, in order:

- *Run to the Mountain: The Story of a Vocation, Vol. 1: 1939–1941*, edited by Patrick Hart, OCSO.

- *Entering the Silence: Becoming a Monk and a Writer, Vol. 2: 1941–1952*, edited by Jonathan Montaldo.

- *A Search for Solitude: Pursuing the Monk's True Life, Vol. 3: 1952–1960*, edited by Lawrence S. Cunningham.

- *Turning Toward the World: The Pivotal Years, Vol. 4: 1960–1963*, edited by Victor A. Kramer.

- *Dancing in the Water of Life: Seeking Peace in the Hermitage, Vol. 5: 1963–1965*, edited by Robert E. Daggy.

- *Learning to Love: Exploring Solitude and Freedom, Vol. 6: 1966*, edited by Christine M. Bochen.

- *The Other Side of the Mountain: The End of the*

Journey, Vol. 7: 1967–1968, edited by Patrick Hart, OCSO.

The editor of this volume, Jon M. Sweeney, has recently published an excellent general introduction to Merton: *Thomas Merton: An Introduction to his Life, Teachings, and Practices*, also available as an audiobook.

Orbis Books has published several books by and about Merton, each of which would assist you in discovering him in other ways:

- *Cold War Letters*, by Thomas Merton. Brings together 111 of the acclaimed Trappist monk's letters to friends, peace activists, artists, and intellectuals—originally distributed in mimeographed form after he was forbidden to publish his thoughts on peace—written between October 1961 and October 1962 at the height of Cold War tensions.

- *Peace in the Post-Christian Era*, by Thomas Merton. Censors of Merton's religious order blocked publication of this work during his lifetime, but a half-century later, despite changing circumstances, his prophetic message remains eerily topical.

- *Living with Wisdom: A Life of Thomas Merton*, by Jim Forest. Absorbing pictorial biography written by the acclaimed peace activist who was also a personal friend of Merton's.

- *The Thomas Merton Encyclopedia*, eds. William H. Shannon, Christine M. Bochen, and Patrick F. O'Connell. The most authoritative essays on 350 topics. Includes fifty illustrations.

- *Thomas Merton: Selected Essays*, ed. Patrick F. O'Connell, foreword by Patrick Hart, OCSO. A broad cross-section of Merton's writings in essay form, from literature to Zen to contemporary politics and activism.

Acknowledgments

The editor and publisher express gratitude for the permission to publish content that originally appeared in the following interviews. They also want to thank Mark Meade and Paul Pearson of the Thomas Merton Center of Bellarmine University, in Louisville, Kentucky, for their kind help and assistance.

Quenon, Paul, OCSO. "'Aware and Awake and Alive': An Interview about Thomas Merton" conducted and edited by George A. Kilcourse, Jr., transcribed by Susan Merryweather. *The Merton Annual* 15 (2002): 210–31. Permission to quote granted by the author.

The editor would also like to express his special thanks to Brother Paul, who added to his original interview a series of further memories of and reflections on living with Fr. Louis, his Novice Master and friend.

Kelly, Timothy OCSO. "'The Great Honesty': Remembering Thomas Merton." Interview by George Kilcourse, edited by Kimberly F. Baker. *The Merton Annual* 9 (1996): 193–220. Permission to quote granted by the author.

Waddell, Chrysogonus OCSO. "Truly Seeking God . . . in Christ." An Interview about Thomas Merton by Victor A. Kramer. *The Merton Annual* 11 (1998): 148–73.

Bamberger, John Eudes OCSO. "Merton's Vocation as a Monastic and Writer." Interview by Victor A. Kramer, edited by Dewey Weiss Kramer. *The Merton Annual* 4 (1991): 21–38.

Kelty, Matthew OCSO. "Looking back to Merton/ Memories and Impressions." Interview by Victor A. Kramer. *The Merton Annual* 1 (1988): 55–76.

Burns, Flavian OCSO. "Merton's Contribution as Teacher, Writer and Community Member." Interview by Victor A. Kramer, edited by Dewey Weiss Kramer. *The Merton Annual* 3 (1990): 71–89.

About the Authors

Brother Paul Quenon, OCSO, entered monastic life in 1958, when he was only seventeen years old. His Novice Master was Thomas Merton, who became an inspiration to Brother Paul as both a writer and photographer. Brother Paul is the author of an award-winning memoir, *In Praise of the Useless Life: A Monk's Memoir*, and many collections of poetry, including *Unquiet Vigil: New and Selected Poems*. Today, Brother Paul still gives talks on Merton, and leads many individuals and groups to discover Merton's life and writings with visits to the hermitage at the Abbey of Gethsemani.

Abbot Timothy Kelly, OCSO, entered monastic life in 1958, and Thomas Merton was his Novice Master. From 1965 until the summer of 1968, he studied canon law in Rome. Returning to the Abbey of Gethsemani, his responsibilities included Master of Novices from 1969 to 1973, and Abbot from 1973 to 2000. Currently he lives and works at the Order's Generalate in Rome, where he serves as Procurator General.

Father Chrysogonus Waddell, OCSO, entered monastic life in 1950, five years before Merton was appointed Novice Master by the Abbot. But he lived with Merton as a fellow monk and friend until Merton's death in 1968. Father Chrysogonus was an internationally respected musician and scholar in the fields of liturgy and Cistercian history. After Merton's death, he lived for decades as a hermit at Gethsemani. He died in 2008.

Father John Eudes Bamberger, OCSO, entered monastic life in 1950, having served in the US Navy and after completing a medical degree. Merton was his Novice Master. He then did a residency in psychiatry at Georgetown University in 1956–57. He left the Abbey of Gethsemani in 1971 when he was elected Abbot at the Abbey of the Genesee, in New York State, and served for more than thirty years. He authored books including *Thomas Merton: Prophet of Renewal*, and his translations of *The Praktikos* and *Chapters on Prayer* by Evagrius Ponticus are still frequently used. He died in 2020.

Father Matthew Kelty, OCSO, entered monastic life in 1960. He was already an ordained priest, had served as a missionary in Papua New Guinea, and worked as an editor of a religious magazine. For a time, he was Merton's personal secretary. He authored several spiritual books and books of collected homilies. He died in 2011.

Father Flavian Burns, OCSO, entered monastic life in 1951. Merton was his Novice Master. After ordination, Fr. Flavian was a student of Canon Law at the Gregorian University in Rome. He was Merton's confessor for a time and was elected Abbot of Gethsemani in the final year of Merton's life, serving from 1968 to 1973, after which he followed Merton into a hermit's life at the monastery. But he would eventually leave for Holy Cross Abbey in Virginia, where he served as Abbot until 1996. He died in 2005.

Jon M. Sweeney is Editor at Large at Orbis Books and author of more than forty books including *The Pope Who Quit*, which was optioned by HBO, *The Complete Francis of Assisi*, *Meister Eckhart's Book of the Heart* (co-authored with Mark S. Burrows), and *Thomas Merton: An Introduction to His Life, Teachings, and Practices*.

Notes

1 *A Search for Solitude: The Journals of Thomas Merton (Vol. 3: 1952–1960)*, ed. Lawrence S. Cunningham; 36, 103. The previous quotation was from p. 19.

2 Paul Elie, *The Life You Save May Be Your Own: An American Pilgrimage* (New York: Farrar, Straus and Giroux, 2004), 292.

3 There are some anecdotes from Brother Patrick sprinkled throughout the forewords and essays he wrote about his old friend, in various books. For instance, there is this one from the foreword to *Selected Essays* by Thomas Merton, ed. Patrick F. O'Connell (Maryknoll, NY: Orbis Books, 2014): "As secretary to Abbot James Fox during the time Merton was novice master, it was my job to deliver to Father Louis the censors' reports, since Dom James preferred not to confront Fr. Louis directly. The latter would mutter such humorous complaints as, 'My God, if you quote the Our Father, the censors would demand a footnote'" (p. vii).

4 "Before I could do it" means writing and publishing poems, and composing and publishing photographs. Since Merton's death, Brother Paul Quenon has become both an accomplished poet and photographer.

5 Brother Paul was only seventeen when he entered

the Abbey of Gethsemani, in 1958. See his memoir *In Praise of the Useless Life: A Monk's Memoir* (Notre Dame, IN: Ave Maria Press, 2018).

[6]"The recollection of this incident in 1958 after his death in 1968 disturbed me. I was inclined to disbelieve it. I was uncertain whether I was remembering something, or just making it up in my imagination—a way of filling in the gaps of what was a sudden and shocking end. His death was terribly significant in many ways, for me a joyful experience, and I felt his presence in a new and closer way" (Brother Paul Quenon).

[7]Dutch-born A. J. Muste (1885–1967) was a Protestant minister and a leading figure in the Pacifist Movement. He was among a number of pacifists, including Daniel and Philip Berrigan, whom Merton invited to his hermitage in 1964 to participate in a retreat on peacemaking.

[8]The author uses the title "Abba" for a fellow novice, and for Merton, in the playful spirit of *Apophthegmata*, remembering two old friends. Desert Fathers were called "Abba," and Desert Mothers, "Amma."

[9]Merton began a correspondence with Etienne Gilson (1884–1978), medieval scholar and professor at the Pontifical Institute of Medieval Studies in Toronto, in 1949 to thank him for *The Spirit of Medieval Philosophy*, which Merton wrote about in his autobiography, *The Seven Storey Mountain*. He wrote that he purchased it at Scribner's bookshop on Fifth Avenue in February 1937 and found in it some of what

drew him toward the Roman Catholic Church. Merton and Gilson then corresponded for many years.

[10]Fr. Barnabas Ahern, CP (1915–95) was a prominent Catholic biblical scholar, the same age as Merton. His obituary in the *New York Times* included this: "During the Second Vatican Council, convened by Pope John XXIII in 1962, Father Ahern collaborated in the drafting of the major texts that re-examined the church's teachings and practices. As the leading American scholar on Scripture at the council, he contributed to the decrees that examined divine revelation, ecumenism and religious freedom" (January 13, 1995).

[11]After graduating from Columbia University, Ernesto Cardenal (1925–2020), the Nicaraguan poet and politician spent two years as a novice at the Abbey of Gethsemani, from 1957 to 1959. Fr. John of the Cross was the monastic name of Edmund Wasserman, who arrived at Gethsemani in 1948 and was a novice under Merton; he too left the monastery—in 1962. "Dom James" refers to the Abbot, Dom James Fox, OCSO (1896–1987).

[12]"The Monk in the Diaspora," published in *Blackfriars*, Vol. 45, July/August 1964, and in Thomas Merton, *Seeds of Destruction* (New York: Farrar, Straus and Giroux, 1964) in the chapter, "The Christian in the Diaspora." Rahner is Karl Rahner (1904–84), the German Jesuit priest and theologian.

[13]There is an excellent article on the Chilean poet Nicanor Parra, his correspondence with Merton in

the late 1960s, and Parra's influence on Merton's experimentation with "anti-poetry": "Poetry of the Sneeze: Thomas Merton and Nicanor Parra," by Paul M. Pearson, *The Merton Journal* 8.2 (Advent 2002): 3–20, http://www.thomasmertonsociety.org/Journal/08/8-2Pearson.pdf.

[14]Where monks who, after a two-year period in the Novitiate (as a novice), having made their "simple vows," will study more in depth before making "solemn vows" and often in preparation for the priesthood as well. This was also sometimes called the Scholasticate.

[15]Father Illtud Evans (1913–72), a Welsh Dominican, born in London, was a convert to Catholicism. He was born John Alban Evans. He was at the Abbey in January 1965.

[16]At this time, the distinction was very clear between the monks who were "Brothers," not on course to become priests, and who spent much more time doing manual work, and "Novices" or Scholastics, who were often studying instead of doing physical work, and preparing to be priests.

[17]Dom Flavian Burns was elected Abbot of the Abbey of Gethsemani in early 1968, after the death of Dom James Fox.